Google Sheets Project: Make a Complete Employee Management System

By

IBNUL JAIF FARABI

Table of Contents

Chapter 1: Introduction

Welcome to "**Google Sheets Project: Make a Complete Employee Management System**". In today's fast-paced world, managing a team effectively is crucial for the success of any organization. Whether you're a small business owner, a team leader, or simply someone looking to streamline your employee management processes, this book is designed to guide you through the creation of a comprehensive employee management system using Google Sheets.

Google Sheets is a powerful, versatile, and free tool that can help you keep track of essential employee information, schedules, attendance, and performance all in one place. Its flexibility allows you to customize your system according to your specific needs, and its ease of use means that even those with little to no experience in spreadsheets can follow along.

This book is structured to take you step-by-step through the process, from setting up the initial spreadsheet to implementing advanced features like conditional formatting and performance tracking. Each chapter is designed to build on the previous one, ensuring that you develop a robust and functional system by the end of the book.

What You Will Learn

- **Setting Up Your Spreadsheet**: We'll start with the basics, including how to create a new Google Sheet, organize employee data, and set up an efficient layout.
- **Managing Employee Shifts**: Learn how to create and manage shift schedules, ensuring that no employee is overworked and that all shifts are covered.
- **Organizing and Formatting Data**: Discover how to freeze rows and columns, merge cells, and apply conditional formatting to make your spreadsheet more user-friendly and visually appealing.
- **Tracking Employee Performance**: Create a performance tracker that uses different colors to represent various types of employee activities, such as Paid Time Off (PTO), Sick Days, and Warnings, and learn how to count and analyze these activities effectively.

Who Is This Book For?

This book is for anyone looking to improve their employee management processes using Google Sheets. Whether you manage a small team, oversee a large department, or are simply looking to enhance your spreadsheet skills, this guide will provide you with the tools and knowledge to create a system that works for you.

Why Google Sheets?

Google Sheets is an excellent choice for creating an employee management system because it is:

- **Free**: Google Sheets is available at no cost, making it an accessible option for businesses of all sizes.
- **Cloud-Based**: Access your data from anywhere, on any device, and collaborate with others in real-time.
- **Flexible**: Google Sheets can be customized to meet your specific needs, from basic data entry to advanced automation and analysis.
- **Integrated**: Easily connect Google Sheets with other Google Workspace tools, such as Google Forms, Google Drive, and Gmail, to create a seamless workflow.

How to Use This Book

This book is designed to be a practical, hands-on guide. Each chapter provides clear, step-by-step instructions, complete with examples and explanations to help you understand the concepts being discussed. I encourage you to follow along with your own Google Sheet as you read, applying what you learn in real-time.

By the end of this book, you will have a fully functional employee management system that you can continue to build upon and customize as your needs evolve. Whether you're just starting out or looking to refine your existing processes, this guide will equip you with the knowledge and skills to succeed.

Let's get started on creating a system that will help you manage your team more efficiently, save time, and reduce stress. Happy managing!

Chapter 2: Getting Started With the Project

Step 1: Create a New Google Sheet

Open Google Sheets: Go to Google Sheets and log in with your Google account.

Create a New Spreadsheet: Click on the blank sheet icon to create a new spreadsheet.

Step 2: Set Up the Employee Information and Schedule Tab

Rename the First Tab: Double-click on the tab name at the bottom (default is "Sheet1") and rename it to "**Employee Information and Schedule**".

Create Headers: In the 10th row, starting from cell A10, enter the following headers:

- Employee Name
- Employee ID
- Department
- Position
- Date of Hire
- Email
- Phone
- Weekly Schedule

Note: We'll put the Weekly Schedule field one row above, because later under this, we're going to add the days of the week underneath this.

Step 3: Format the Header Row

Select the Header Row: Click and drag to select the first row.

Bold and Center Align: Click on the Bold button (B) and the Center Align button in the toolbar to format the headers.

Then, don't forget to select the entire sheet, wrap the sheet, so that everything looks neat and pretty. You can use wrap like this → Format > Wrapping > Wrap

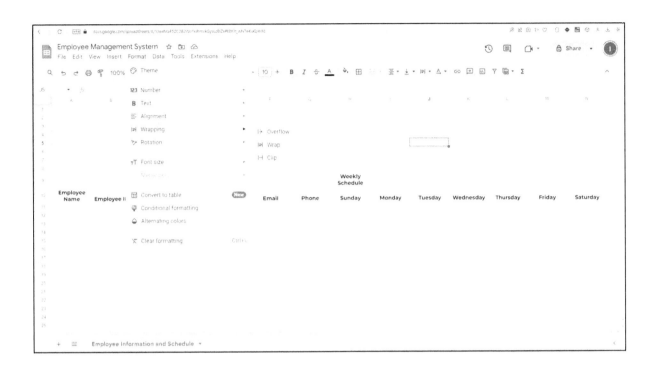

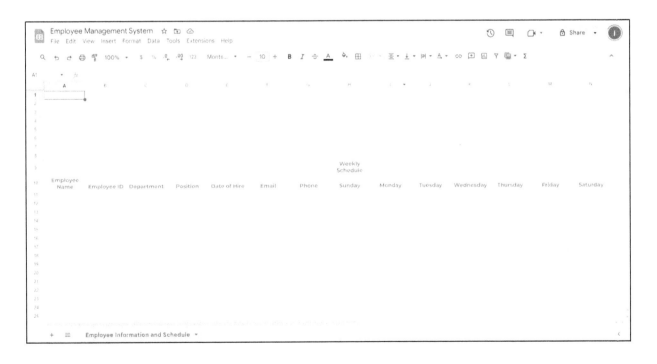

Chapter 3: Entering the Data

Step 1: Entering employee data

Start entering your employee data under each header. Here's the list of employee names.

- Michael Johnson
- Emily Davis
- Christopher Miller
- Jessica Wilson
- Matthew Brown
- Sarah Moore
- Joshua Taylor
- Ashley Anderson
- Andrew Thomas
- Megan Martin

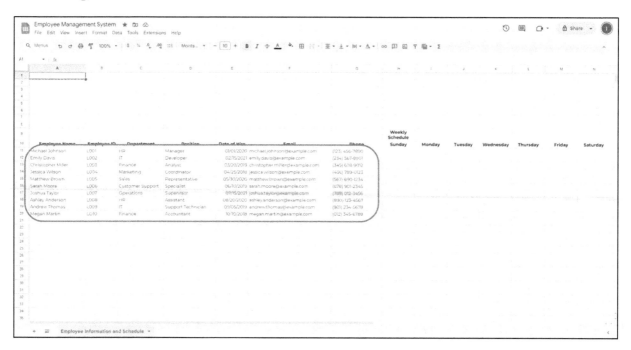

Step 2: Creating and Managing Employee Shifts

Then we will set up a system to manage employee shifts in Google Sheets. We'll ensure that each employee works no more than 5 shifts a week and schedule them according to the three defined shifts:

- Shift A: 6 AM - 4 PM
- Shift B: 4 PM - 12 AM
- Shift C: 12 AM - 8 AM

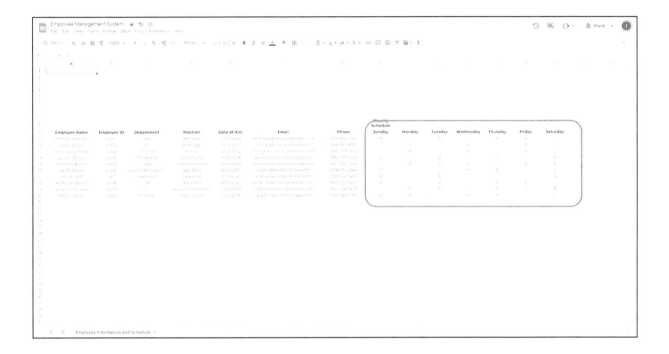

Then we need to be sure that no employee works more than 5 shifts in a week (Sunday - Saturday), so we'll need to calculate total shifts per employee per week.

The employee "Michael Johnson", who's on row 11, we can calculate the total shifts per week by using this formula.

= COUNTA(H11:N11)

Then we'll apply for the rest of the employees. After entering the formula in cell O11, drag the fill handle down from O11 to O20 to apply the formula to all employees. This will automatically update the range for each row, ensuring each employee's total shifts are counted accurately.

The **COUNTA** function counts the number of cells that contain any type of data, including text, numbers, dates, and logical values. In our shift schedule, each cell within a row (from Sunday to Saturday) contains either a shift code (A, B, or C) or is left blank if the employee is not scheduled to work that day.

Here, we want to ensure that each employee works no more than 5 shifts per week. To achieve this, we use the **COUNTA** function to count the number of shifts assigned to each employee. The function **COUNTA** will count the non-empty cells in the range.

Chapter 4: Freezing Rows and Columns, Merging Cells and Applying Conditional Formatting

Step 1: Freezing Rows

I'd like to freeze up to certain rows, so that if we scroll, the data in those rows will remain static. We want to make sure that the headers always remain on the screen, so we'll freeze until row 10.

First select the row 10, then click on **View >> Freeze >> Up to row 10**.

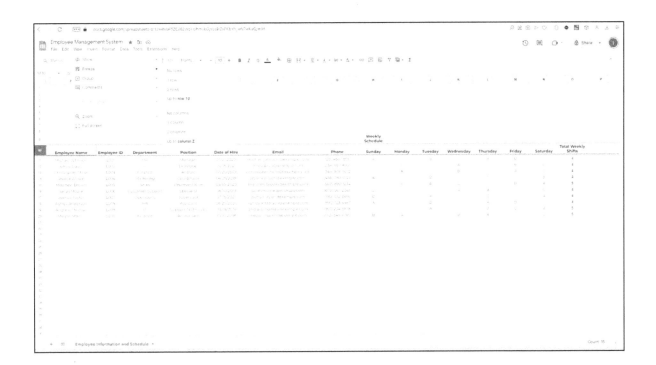

Step 2: Freezing Columns

Next, I'll freeze the Employee Name column, so that it always stays on the screen, even when we start scrolling to the right.

First select column A, then click on **View >> Freeze >> Up to column A**.

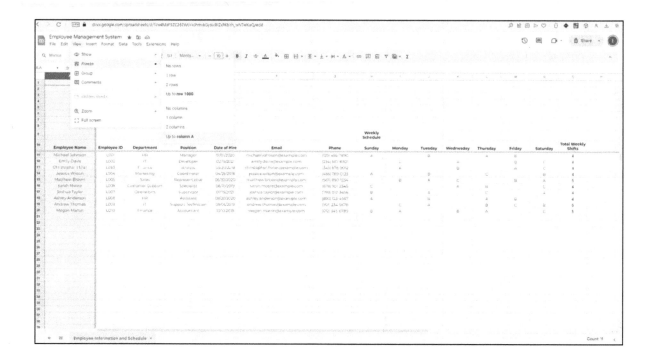

Step 3: Merging Cells

We should make sure that the Weekly Schedule header spans all the days of the week, so we need to merge cells H9 through O9. We should select those cells first, then click **Format >> Merge cells >> Merge all.**

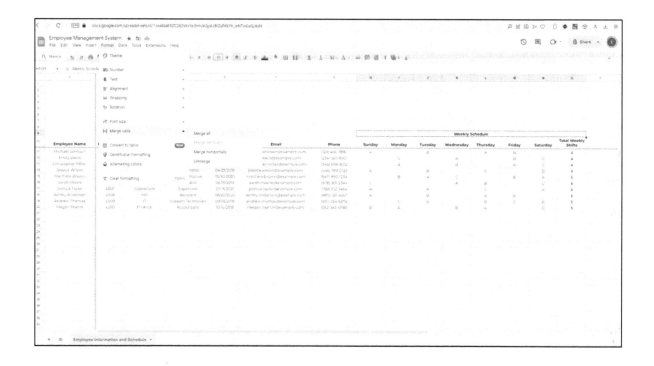

Step 4: Conditional Formatting

Now we'll apply conditional formatting to differentiate between shifts. This visual aid will help in quickly identifying which shift each employee is scheduled for by using different colors for each shift.

We can select columns H though N (Sunday - Saturday). This'll be the range where we'll apply the conditional formatting. With the range selected, we can go to **Format >> Conditional Formatting**.

Set the Rule for Shift A:

Under the "Format cells if" drop-down menu, select "Text is exactly".

In the text box, enter A.

Choose the Formatting Style:

Click on the "Formatting style" box to choose the color. For Shift A, you might choose a light green color.

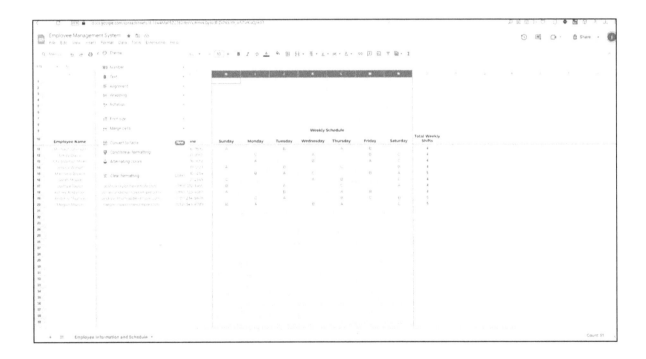

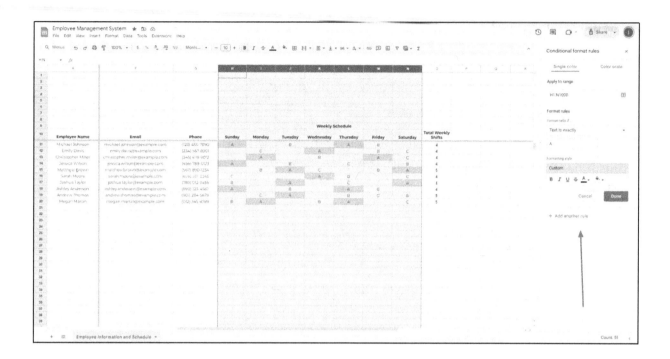

Now, you can start adding conditional formatting for shifts B and C. You can click on "Add another rule" in the Conditional formatting rules panel.

Set the Rule for Shift B:

Under the "Format cells if" drop-down menu, select "Text is exactly".

In the text box, enter B.

Choose the Formatting Style:

Click on the "Formatting style" box to choose the color. For Shift B, you might choose a light blue color.

Set the Rule for Shift C:

Under the "Format cells if" drop-down menu, select "Text is exactly".

In the text box, enter C.

Choose the Formatting Style:

Click on the "Formatting style" box to choose the color. For Shift C, you might choose a light orange color.

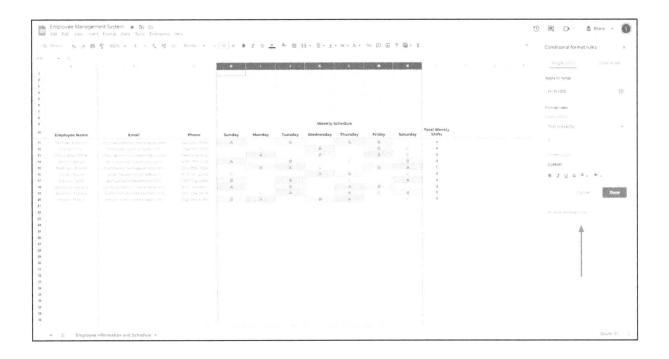

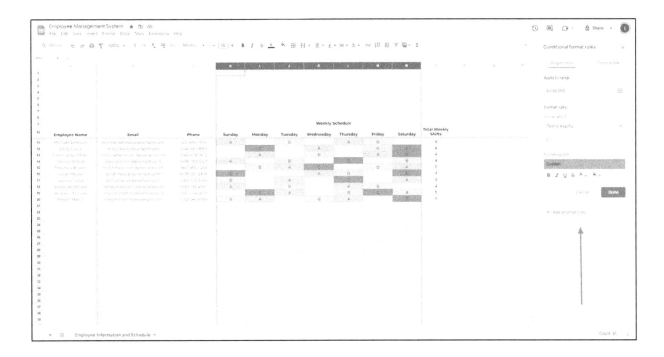

Step 5: Change Fill Colors for the Headers

Now, we can change the fill colors for the different headers.

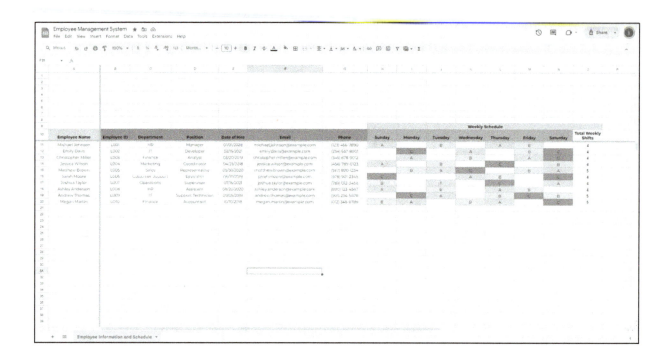

Now we can add a title for the whole sheet. We can write "**Employee Information and Schedule**" on B2 and then merge all the cells through B2 and G5. We can hold the Shift key on the keyboard to select multiple cells easily.

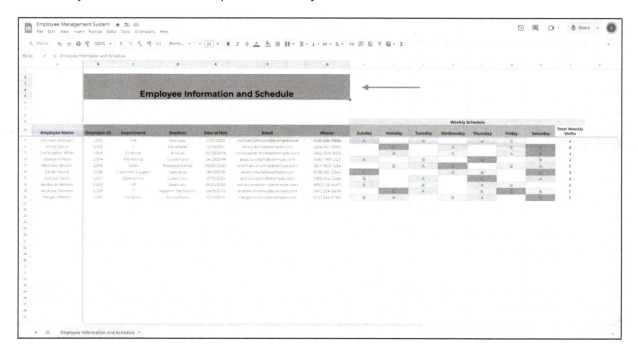

Now we can create a legend for shift information which will provide information about the different shifts and their corresponding colors.

First write the "**Shift Information**" on cell I2, then merge all the cells through I2 to K2.

Write "Shift A" on cell C3, the shift hours "8 AM – 4 PM" on cell J3 and fill cell K3 with light green color which identifies that Shift A is light green.

Write "Shift B" on cell C4, the shift hours "4 PM – 12 AM" on cell J4 and fill cell K4 with light blue color which identifies that Shift B is light blue.

Write "Shift C" on cell C5, the shift hours "12 AM – 8 AM" on cell J5 and fill cell K5 with light orange color which identifies that Shift C is light orange.

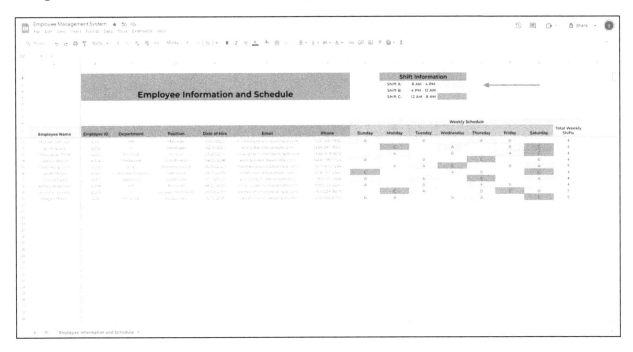

Now, we'll add the borders in the respective areas to properly identify them.

We can add borders to the "**Employee Information and Schedule**" part by clicking on cell B2 (cell B2 is merged through cell G5) and click on the "Borders" from the toolbar.

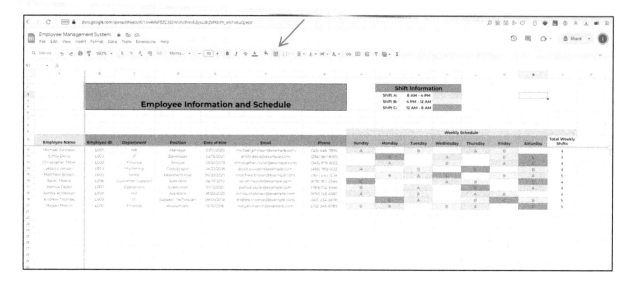

We can add borders to the employee table by selecting cells A10 through Q20. We can first click cell A10, then click and press the Shift button, then click cell Q20, and that'll allow us to select multiple cells at once.

Then border the "**Weekly Schedule**" part cell H9 (cell H9 is merged through cell O9).

Finally, add border to the "**Shift Information**" part by selecting cells I2 through K5.

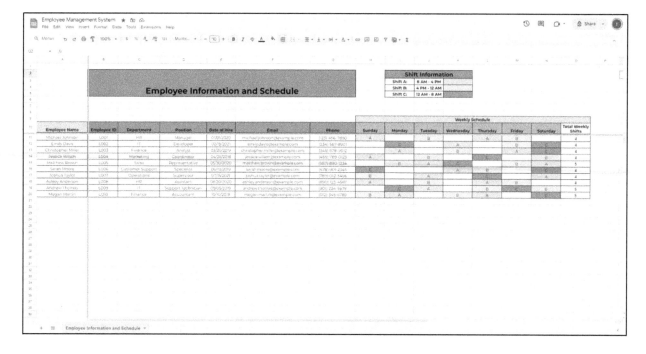

Chapter 5: Creating a Performance Tracker with Conditional Formatting

In this chapter, we will create a new sheet that tracks employee performance during a week in August, 2024, using different colors for various types of keys such as Paid Time Off (PTO), Unpaid Time Off (UTO), Sick (S), and others. We will also count the occurrences of each type for every employee.

First, we can create a new sheet and rename it to "**Employee Performance**".

We'll include the following keys.

- PTO - Paid Time Off
- UTO - Unpaid Time Off
- S - Sick
- SS - Shift Swapped
- CO - Call-Out
- NCNS - No Call No Show
- VW - Verbal Warning
- WW - Written Warning

First, add the employee names in column A, the Employee Name header in cell A12 and the names from cell A13 through A22.

We can write "**Employee Performance**" as the sheet title on B2 and then merge all the cells through B2 and H2. We can hold the Shift key on the keyboard to select multiple cells easily. We can fill the cells with the pink color.

Now we'll add the different types of keys as the legend underneath the title. We can write "Performance Keys" on cell B4 then merge all the cells through B4 and H4. Underneath this, we can add different types of keys and their colors.

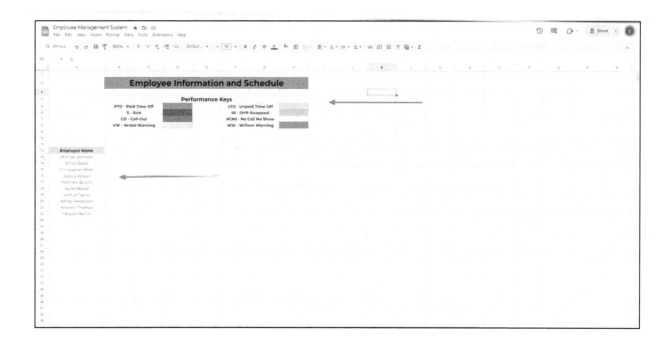

Now, we need to add the dates and the days of the week.

First, we need to add the dates. On cell B12, we can write "8/4/2024" and make sure it's a date by selecting the **Format >> Number >> Date** option. Then we drag cell B12 through H12 and it'll automatically increment the dates, so cell H12 will be the date "8/10/2024".

On top of it, we can add the days of the week. On cell B11, we can write "Sunday". Then we drag cell B11 through H11 and it'll automatically increment the days, so cell H11 will be the date "Saturday".

On top of it, we can write "**Week of 8/4/2024 - 8/10/2024**" on cell B10 then merge all the cells through B10 and H10.

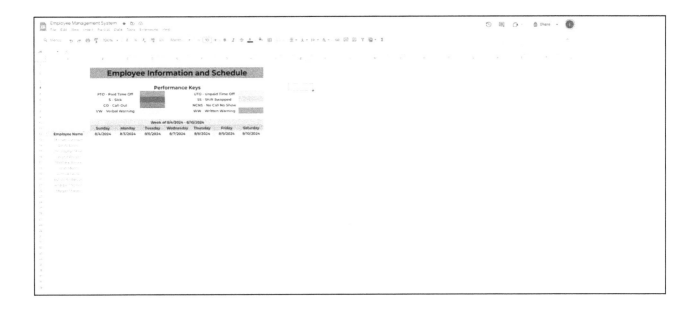

Now we need to add different types of column headers for calculating different types of keys.

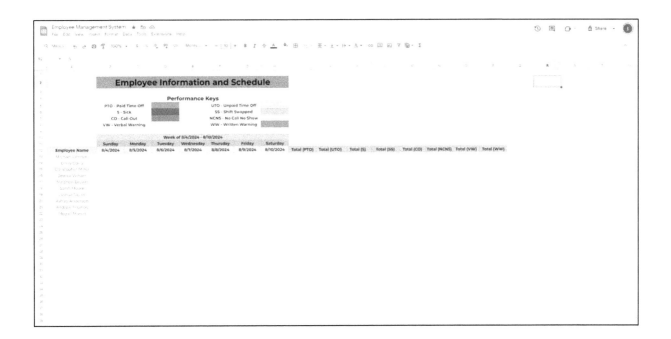

Now, we can add the data for each employee for the week.

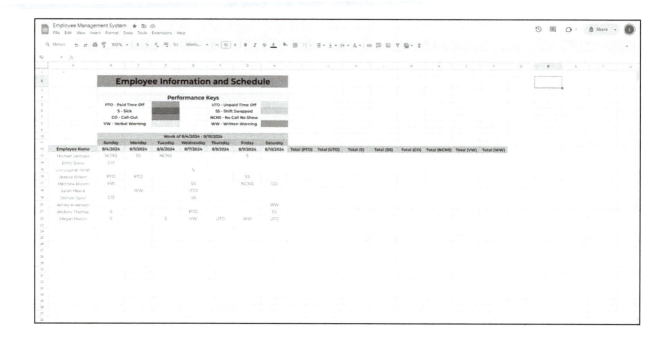

Now we'll apply conditional formatting to differentiate between keys. This visual aid will help in quickly identifying the performance key for each employee by using different colors for each key.

We can select columns B though H (8/4/2024, Sunday - 8/10/2024, Saturday). This'll be the range where we'll apply the conditional formatting. With the range selected, we can go to **Format >> Conditional Formatting**.

Set the Rule for performance key "PTO":

Under the "Format cells if" drop-down menu, select "Text is exactly".

In the text box, enter PTO.

Choose the Formatting Style:

Click on the "Formatting style" box to choose the color. For Shift A, you might choose the specific color.

Then repeat it for the rest of the keys.

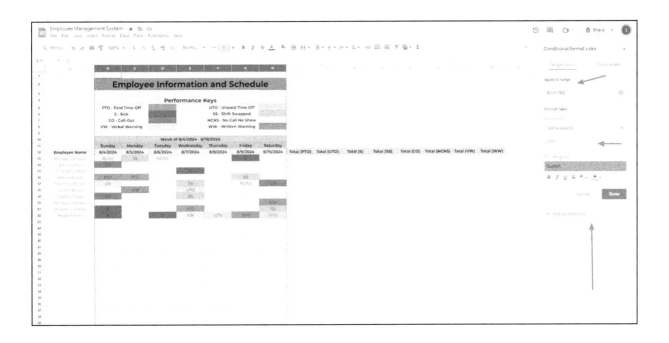

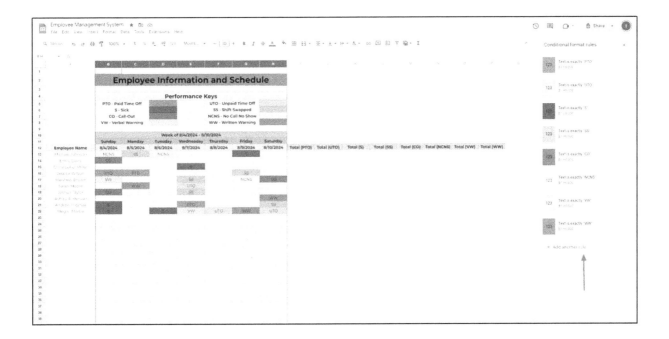

Now, we need to count the different types of keys for the week.

For "**PTO**", on cell I13, we can use the formula "= COUNTIF(B13:H13, "PTO")". Then drag the cell I13 through cell I22, and it'll apply the formula from cell I13 all the way through I22 for respective rows.

For "**UTO**", in cell J13, use the formula "= COUNTIF(B13:H13, "UTO")". Then, drag cell J13 through cell J22 to apply the formula from cell J13 through J22.

For "**S**", in cell K13, use the formula "= COUNTIF(B13:H13, "S")". Drag cell K13 through cell K22 to apply the formula from cell K13 through K22.

For "**SS**", in cell L13, use the formula "= COUNTIF(B13:H13, "SS")". Drag cell L13 through cell L22 to apply the formula from cell L13 through L22.

For "**CO**", in cell M13, use the formula "= COUNTIF(B13:H13, "CO")". Drag cell M13 through cell M22 to apply the formula from cell M13 through M22.

For "**NCNS**", in cell N13, use the formula "= COUNTIF(B13:H13, "NCNS")". Drag cell N13 through cell N22 to apply the formula from cell N13 through N22.

For "**VW**", in cell O13, use the formula "= COUNTIF(B13:H13, "VW")". Drag cell O13 through cell O22 to apply the formula from cell O13 through O22.

For "**WW**", in cell P13, use the formula "= COUNTIF(B13:H13, "WW")". Drag cell P13 through cell P22 to apply the formula from cell P13 through P22.

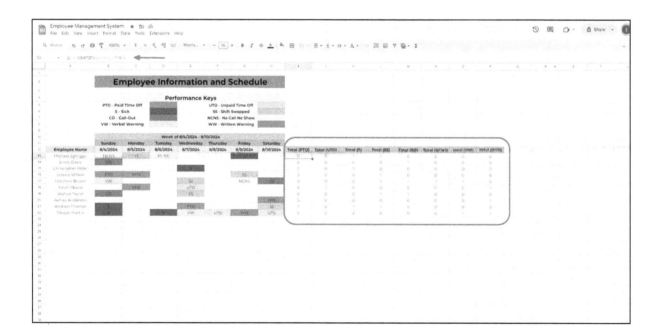

Now, we can add the borders to the specific cells.

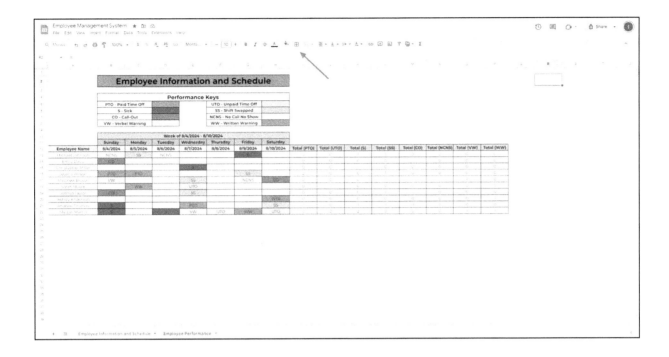

Employee Information and Schedule

Performance Keys

PTO - Paid Time Off		UTO - Unpaid Time Off	
S - Sick		SS - Shift Swapped	
CO - Call-Out		NCNS - No Call No Show	
VW - Verbal Warning		WW - Written Warning	

Week of 8/4/2024 - 8/10/2024

Employee Name	Sunday 8/4/2024	Monday 8/5/2024	Tuesday 8/6/2024	Wednesday 8/7/2024	Thursday 8/8/2024	Friday 8/9/2024	Saturday 8/10/2024	Total (PTO)	Total (UTO)	Total (S)	Total (SS)	Total (CO)	Total (NCNS)	Total (VW)	Total (WW)
	NCNS	SS	NCNS												
	SS														
	PTO	PTO				SS									
	VW					NCNS	CO								
		WW		UTO											
				SS											
							WW								
				PTO			SS								
				VW	UTO	WW	UTO								

Chapter 6: Conclusion

Thank you for joining me on this journey through "**Google Sheets Project: Make a Complete Employee Management System**". We've covered the essential steps needed to create, manage, and maintain a functional employee management system using Google Sheets. Whether you're a small business owner, a team leader, or someone interested in enhancing your spreadsheet skills, I hope this book has provided you with the knowledge and confidence to build your own system.

Managing employees can be a complex task, but with the right tools, it becomes much more manageable. Google Sheets offers a powerful and flexible platform that can centralize your employee data, track schedules, monitor performance, and ensure everything runs smoothly. Throughout this book, we've broken down the process into easy-to-follow steps, from setting up basic employee information to creating detailed performance trackers with conditional formatting.

Key Takeaways:

- **Getting Started**: We began by setting up a basic spreadsheet, entering employee information, and organizing data into a readable format.
- **Managing Shifts**: We explored how to set up and manage employee shifts, ensuring no employee works more than the allotted number of shifts per week. We also used functions like COUNTA to automate the counting process.
- **Organizing Data**: Freezing rows and columns, merging cells, and applying conditional formatting helped us create a more user-friendly and visually organized system. These steps ensure that important data is always visible, and that shifts are easily distinguishable by color.
- **Tracking Performance**: Finally, we developed a performance tracker that uses conditional formatting to visually represent different performance keys. We counted occurrences of various performance metrics, giving a clear overview of each employee's activities.

Moving Forward:

With this system in place, you now have a solid foundation for managing your team's information and activities in an organized, efficient manner. Google Sheets' capabilities extend far beyond what we've covered in this book, so I encourage you to explore further. Consider integrating additional features like automated email notifications, advanced data analysis, or even connecting your sheet to other Google Workspace tools.

This book is just the beginning of what you can achieve with Google Sheets. As you grow more comfortable with the platform, you'll discover countless ways to customize and enhance your employee management system to fit your unique needs.

Thank you for your time and effort in following along with this guide. I hope it serves you well in your role as a manager, team leader, or spreadsheet enthusiast. Remember, the key to success lies not just in the tools you use, but in how effectively you use them. Keep learning, keep exploring, and continue to build systems that work for you and your team.

Good luck, and happy managing!